SOME LATE ADVENTURE OF THE FEELINGS

MISFIT

Lynn,

I've said it, but
it more than bears
writing down — Dorothy
L'Amour had me, dozens
of times, reeling with
astonishment, pleasure,
excitement. If I do that
even once here I'll be thrilled.

Mark.

SOME LATE ADVENTURE OF THE FEELINGS

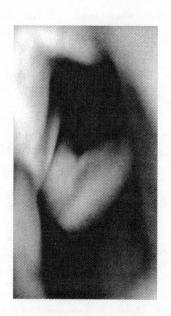

poems by MARK SINNETT

MISFIT

ECW PRESS

CANADIAN CATALOGUING IN PUBLICATION DATA

Sinnet, Mark, 1963–
Some late adventure of the feelings

Poems.
a misFit book
ISBN 1-55022-410-7

I. Title.

PS8587.IS63S65 2000   C811'.54   C00-930443-6
PR9199.3.S5356865 2000

A misFit book edited by Michael Holmes
Cover and text design by Tania Craan
Cover image by Hanne Godtfeldt
Author photo by Samantha Mussells
Layout by Mary Bowness
Printed by Marc Veullieux

Distributed in Canada by General Distribution Services,
325 Humber Blvd., Toronto, Ontario M9W 7C3

Published by ECW PRESS
2120 Queen Street East, Suite 200,
Toronto, Ontario, M4E IE2
www.ecw.ca/press

The publication of *Some Late Adventure of the Feelings* has been generously
supported by The Canada Council, the Ontario Arts Council,
and the Government of Canada through the Book Publishing
Industry Development Program.   Canada

TABLE OF CONTENTS

ACKNOWLEDGEMENTS

My thanks to Jack David, Hanne Godtfeldt, Steven Heighton, Joanna Lyon, and Samantha Mussells. There would be no book without them. Special thanks to my editor and friend Michael Holmes.

I am also grateful to The Ontario Arts Council.

A few of these poems appeared in *The New Quarterly*. My thanks to Mary Merikle. More are slated for *The Fiddlehead*.

For Sam, every word

ART HISTORY

I've tried in any number of complicated and winding ways
to get down a little of what it is, this happening's core.
Tortured myself two days with dull metaphor, duller
and anxious nights; staggered back in rooms well-lit
and populated, demanding, and others not so bright,
from your knowing and significant image looming in,
though not alarmingly. That vision is embroidered,
I realize, with other more quick-cut details of our passing
through each other's orbit: the back of your arm reaching up,
breath catching in you sharply, then less so, the small
and warm small of your back, your arching at planets
unnamed as the long night comes strangely unhooked
from time's needle. I have even made monkish passage
through libraries, haunting, for a morning, the work
of others similarly afflicted. And discovered in Modigliani's
Reclining Nude, 1917, for instance, a similar abandon,
or if not that, then a slow dissolving of resolve, the presence
of something off-camera that might be welcomed, however
briefly, into the invisible frame. (Though his couch is dark
rather than light, and the woman, to be honest, not even
your pale imitation, having none of the disarming gestures,
nor your fleet route into memory.) And somewhere
further along was Turner's *Woman Reclining on a Couch*.
It is a far remove from the massed and blazing skies
of London, but I understood in fragments (without ever
believing I could put that knowledge down, entrap it)
what he was after with that frumpy interior. And how
some mornings even grey smoke pouring under, piling up
this side of his door, wouldn't interest him, such wild
conflagration was there in his blind and thumping heart.

HYMN

The hills behind this rented house
are sunstruck, nothing more,
but I choose to believe fires have broken out
in the tops of trees;
that a hundred blazes rush
into each other's arms

and flare-ups in fields of sugar cane
cause toffee to rush molten
down the lane, set hard over books
left poolside, over swooning red flags
of hibiscus.

There is also, undeniably,
the blunt, stomachy bleat of goats,
and a woolly patter and blanket of rain
falls onto their backs from the variegated sky.

A woman somewhere up there
sings along to spirituals on the radio,
her voice that of a siren.

There is no disproving any of this
unless I go after them, brave the ill-tempered dogs,
the blue heat and steeplechasing rain,
abandon you here, leave you
unguarded. Which is unthinkable.

Because even sighting God in that woman's home,
top of the slope, tapping his foot
and rhapsodizing, taking a bright moment,

or even *gods*, grouped around

some star-bright karaoke machine,
littering the shade with empties,
and listening to each other, rapt, heads back,
under slick umbrella palm

is no match for you, love,
padding my way, your eyes
full still of a tropical sleep, the half-memory of dreams,
strange subterranean translations
of what I've heard and written down here,

and the possibility, if I stay, of us
rifling together this strange kitchen
for lost coffee beans, your hip brushing past my hand,
the kettle fogging us in.

SUNDAY

Dawn, and stands of fire-swept birch
are congregated off-road.

They are burnt-out limbo dancers, I see that,
all black leg and brown belly, high white
blouses. Thin arms held in the air.

This is so easy a move from the literal,
no leap. Just the wind-slapped plainness of it
against the sky as I urge the flatbed along
soft red roads.

No way, though, with the mind so sleep-dead
and all the graphite impressions rising in me
monotonal, monstrous, to get it down.

How clearly, regardless, I saw them,
their new ghost-life. A lean crowd
of symbols burnt into the world,
its high alpine mind-clearing,
but elusive and so camera-shy.

Then begin again:
Sam and what she means.
The beyond-science reach and cling of those
humming synapse highwires.

Well, top of the rise and seven a.m.
it's that clear, as lucid with me:
I see a rail-thin crowd in crazy
halter tops, standing tall
and grooving into daylight.

STATE

At one point this morning (sun flooding
a coffee shop, its chopped-up Edward Hoppers,
the leaning akimbo and salt-stained floors)
the world resolved unexpectedly, didn't loom
so heavily. Another dimension, it felt, had been
hinted at, teased up somehow from the day's
white scalp. This state is so rare for me
that when it comes there is the sense
of an altogether better life frequency
moving laser-like through the atmosphere.
The inhibiting physical properties of air
are nonexistent. All the barriers are
unnecessary for a minute or two, an hour.
But the trouble with a sense of interior space
(knowing vividly the way thoughts are
always being made, put together inside;
having heard and even felt the electric
chemicals welling up, bursting forth)
is that there is so little hope of that
small-grain resolution lasting very long,
the supple-soft lucidity. But today, with this
room awash in lemon-yellow light, air unhurriedly
passing over all of us, and a good silence being offered up
between songs, there was enough time for me to see
how S. has become sewn already into myriad circuits
and set above all temporary things.
I recognized that she is wholly responsible
for all the unheard joys tunnelling away,
and is probable cause of this focused interlude,
precious alone but doubly so for floating up
such buoyant truths that might harden before
this gallant though cool and dying sun.

AGAIN, WITH FEELING

It happens in a lifetime over and again —
without knowing, it is the last time.

A restaurant frequented and then
inexplicably forgotten. Or else bright affection
touches no more the deeper, leaping
and skittish places in the body.
The last morning together.

But it's not thoughts of a final day
doing me in here; that sky will loom
and blaze however petulant my stomping,
how well-wrought the fury.

Rather, chaos inhabits me, jostles most
when I recall the hesitant and breathtaking
ways you revealed to night-blue air
such complicated physics and gentle expressions,
and then consider it might never happen again.

I would in an instant, offered the means,
revive the exquisite graces of that night
so they might configure themselves
over time in the infinite variations
required of evolution.

And would perhaps, since all is hazard,
begin with this: Your arm, lift it, move it up
again behind your head that way you do,

then pray it happens.

FUEL

You stood at the window
gathering the lemon drape
into its high black waist,

were foreground to a full-frame
pottery blue and the skyward
rush of root and bulb,

the purple thrust, furred heart
of early crocus. Our winter
bones, I said, have begun

their retreat into the body's
slow marrow. May's heat
has come back for us,

reached through unseen mazes
to touch us dead centre.
But none of this out loud.

I touched your shoulder,
played that way for time,
for better nerve. All our moves

were a heat-softened tumble
through linen drifts,
great glaciers of sheet.

The new season's warm air
limboed under the sash
(that white pine board

in heaven's floor), worked up

our legs. Its cells wrestled,
tumbled head over heels,

just as we did. It was
the invisible version of us
and we breathed it as fuel,

as permission to feast within
evening's soft new angles,
bronze in its orange fire.

STUDY OF TWO FIGURES (LOVERS), 1846

There is nothing in Millet's red chalk drawing,
its round tumbling lines, to suggest the couple
is indoors, and yet I place them, predictably,
in a room that reminds me of yours, and decide they are
like us — so often and for such long stretches
of these unforgettable and wise-seeming days
are we also undraped. Even so, I doubt there is
any sign of blue velour, or leopard prints, your
glistening black pants, in the rough shamble
of clothes beyond the frame's limit. More
possible, I guess, is a small and familiar tangle
of soft velvet gloves like those I have seen on your
kitchen counter. And that when Millet is done
they might climb again, like bright bunched-up
caterpillars, the woman's unfinished arms.
The man's head (I appreciate most especially
this detail, his desire, I'm drawn to the work
because of it) rests easily on her bare shoulder.
She sits at his feet, but as an equal; it is not
a position that should be read as difficult. Her
cheek is against his leg, her arm furthermore
drapes over it, hangs free and languorous.
I realize if the hand were drawn in fully
it would ghost Marat's death, a notion that has me
riffing away to linked but recent true poems
by a friend, as well as the lurid collage next to
your fridge. This frail chain seems, end of the day,
giveaway evidence of chaos theory, its tiger's reach
through some hundred and fifty years. But
the two figures touch me, is how this adds up, all
it means, and they do it delicately, just as you do:
back of the neck and with the tip of your tongue.

CUBA

We've talked about this (which stuns me,
to find that my history now contains a few
angular and emerald moments of ours),
about not being able to bring you readily,
at all hours, to mind; not wanting that power
anyway. It means I recognize the atomic limits
of a mind, adore in fact its failings and the dizzy
anticipation it makes out of being apart. That short
in the system, the sudden and maddening cable
outage, seems sign of a purest physics. But this
phenomenon — your reduction on the inside screen
to static, a staggering turn you made gone awry
and pointillist, for instance — also drives me, or would
eventually, to airports lit with desire and a series
of descended screens that flutter, click with green
and luminous mentions of Havana, the furnace
sands of Varadero. I would come to you. And even
settle, if doing so would make in any way my arrival
before you possible (and that arrival welcome), all
the long-drawn bar tabs, make right the unforgivable
debts. This ambition, now spoken, will keep me
awake nights, flutter at me like an alarm.
Or a bright bird I might later present to you,
claiming with solemn nods and a believing heart
that I have taught it everything: all the elaborate
blue talk of sailors and the words of better poets,
as well as how to swoop and arc, plummet and dive
in an impossible routine that leaves your name
written indelibly along the equator's blank line.

VITAMINS

A walk in the city makes less impression lately, upstairs
is so full of electric moments, and recent days teem
with engraved and brilliant scenes. The limestone details
fade, as well as all the nineteenth-century enhancements
and aggravations so often and needlessly uppermost.
Today the reason is angular thoughts of a sherbet green
T-shirt, your tan arms below twin lime horizons. And also
what it means to have lingered a minute with you, musing
on ideas that won't soon shatter any long-held notions but
still passed between us like a series of kisses. Who
in the world would want to rush that? Also enduring are
the silver attachments: through your tongue, and bright
softer spirals slipped over fingers. Your painted toes.
Evenings lately I have seen, from the green back and forth
of your eyes, how you read films, and noted quick shifts
in the air's makeup when you move my way — against
an arm or a shoulder that will hum, its every atom roused.
While we sleep my watchband occasionally circles your rings
on the desk like a metal fence. And this morning you sorted
vitamins — some high dosage C, some potassium and zinc,
as well as herbal and less specific supplements. I took them
gladly but, truth is, my days are full: of sweet extravagant fruit,
the winter sun streaming over a shared *Globe*, deep-night
tumblers of scotch, and your breath feathering my cheek.
Nothing, love, will keep me better than these.

PLAINSONG

To put it plainly, and leaving the word tangles, the headache
syntax out of this one (though I'll have to burn it maybe,
after you've seen it, find a delight in how ashes ascend
from the remains like the darkest, most ragged and drunken
moths, rather than in its complications, and knowing
full well that with this tactic I run the risk of a piece sentimental
and mawkish, an ode which might do in the reputation, run counter
to a good grain, a plum vein long worked and sanded down
until it means everything to me, its whorling smooth and illustrative
surface), I have to say this: When you entered the café today, not
long after lunch, and me deep into a decent novel that transported me
back fifty years (though in the protagonist's dire money straits and
the yellowed Penguin pages I must admit I saw bits of yesterday,
and the several weeks before), all upright about the shoulders
and with a smile banned in half the world, so bright and
endangering to drivers less than splendid, Formula One, as well
as cataract victims, airline pilots, I was knocked back as it struck me
so clearly how beautiful you are. And not for the first time. How
that means in everything you do and not just in the way you move,
black-platformed and knowingly, electrically across any room.
And how, given absolutely anyone in the world walking towards me
right then I'd have turned all but you away. Said, Thanks
but it's Sam I'm waiting on, it will always be her, given
the choice, the right words and her feeling the same way.

WISHFUL

I would see you in all the doorways, it's that bad.
Or at traffic lights, waiting. And in restaurants

absorbed by talk of malt whisky, behind glass
reflective and resistant to my hopeful and hopeless

passing. I would see you springing lightly
from gunmetal 4-runner, headed either for

art gallery or run-down bookstore. In any
of these places, gladly, and in all others here

forgotten. Most obviously, I would have you
there only momentarily, waylaid and heading

in all the dramatic instances my way. I would
see you. (Though in your hundred blunt

refusals to appear this way I recognize
limits that never before concerned me.)

PAUSE

A comma missing from the last line of your note
has my attention. Love me, it says, bottom of a page
full of alternatives for an evening that shapes up just fine,
whatever we choose. Which is clever stuff, that ending,
it pumps adrenalin (and whatever else from the elemental
table dizzies a man, cinches him immediately, tightly about
the chest) in quantities reserved in the normal course
for first-time parasailers, hepped-up jitterbugs. And I do,
you know. Would lavish, in fact, all attention on you,
buy up the world's headlines if it would help.
This afternoon (hands on my old Seiko moving in
torturously slow fashion, and knowing that somewhere
in the city you were breathing a few atoms into bright
art-clad rooms that contain more than is possible
to log in a life, some reduced and yet still mysterious worlds,
but offer up no sight or sound of me — though a few
memories, the slight influence of a morning shared
mostly and well) I recalled, with a clarity that surprised
me, my first apprehension of you: in a gallery and
talking to a man who wore glasses and couldn't hold
completely your interest. Your right hand scratched
idly at the small of your back and I listened for
the noise from that gesture. The memory (or rather
its effect on the all the sympathetic and intermittently
nervous systems) makes your unpunctuated request
so damn easy to answer. But again, that curling hair,
the absent wet comma. I could use it. Would carry it
in my wallet like a photo of you, haul it everywhere
and faithfully, as elegant proof we contain, us two, the same
time-stopping truth: mutual aims might give us long pause.

WHAT IT IS FLOODS

Beautiful to be able to sit, write a few
unhurried and nearly lazy lines. To do
not much more than cast words lightly
at the paper, have them arrive on the breath

rather than try very hard to leave anything
indelible. But most of all to know that,
two days on, and breaking recent pattern,
I will see you reading them. And as your eyes

dart left at a line break, or inch right,
(or as your breath shifts this gentle
and glad poem through an inch or two
of clean coastal air), my brain will hum

electric, be moved from its regular mooring
place at the sight and daunting
proximity of you. Tonight, still most of
a country removed, I know already how

I will want to feel exactly what it is floods
through you, seeing me opposite again. Or
failing that, would have these words bring you
across the room's dividing space into mine,

that forever and wherever adores you,
and in which I will have carved room
enough for both of us, so long as we
stay close. A shoulder of yours pressed

to my lips should serve well, and perhaps a
brown hand cradling another's hip, all the
extra words abandoned to sweet darkness
and the desperate empty months behind us.

TRIGGERS

Saddest thing — now that the grandest sadness
ebbs a bit, and realization dawns that neither of us
will fail this test, or fade away —
must be the reminders of you
everywhere I go.

Though even as I put the notion down
it threatens
                    to turn on me,
become something not maudlin at all,
but the jade and inlaid trigger
to a host of memories I wouldn't trade.

The mangos, for instance. Piled, and climbing all over
each other, red-faced and olive-green
at every second store
(and in the fridge now).

Or obscure tunes shared months back,
and other end of Lake Ontario,
but that have made their way here
                                        and spill
from car windows, as well as from wrought iron
and wave-pattern patios
like rainbow trout. Their metal ghosts
leak atomically from Walkmans.

There are these too: Bricks of seeded soap
the likes of which I would smell on you
again or, after your shower,
inspect for the soft print of your hand,
                                        the arc
and round resistance of your shoulders.

There is also, I suppose, the food I choose
now to put in my body, or choose

                not to.

And the way Ryan all weekend was saying,
Did you see *her?*
And I never did, but was glad to have him say it
because your presence rose in me

                at those moments

like a rush of proof in the blood.

PUZZLES

How to tell her when I tell her
she is beautiful

that I have picked the wrong word,
so clearly would that one seem to
cling only to her skin

or to tangle its syllables
in her hair, flit bat-like and simple
over her hands and wondrous arms.

How to suggest without seeming to
suggest some complex nuclear medicine
or obscure religious vista

that what I have in mind hunts deeper,
and I sense in her a place and a state
should be marked on all the grand
original maps.

And finally (this is hardest)
how to confess plainly
that I haven't found those better words,
sounds which might describe her
effect on this world

and in a café this week, her hand
a careening second on my arm,
I knew it might take years.

LONG DISTANCE

Yesterday I got your message and it felt necessary
to sit, jot a few words on how you wanting to leave me
the sound of your voice — and then doing that, making a gift
of its modulations and proximity — struck me, and still does, a day on,
as the best gift, in both its intention and execution, I can
remember. So damn filling of the soul, and also gloriously sad
in the identical instant, like opera, or first albums by The Cure,
or Joy Division, and these days Buckley, the atoms switching
sides, an alternating emotional current. You should know I
rewound, replayed your words; damn near wore the tape clear
through. Hard to describe or imagine exactly how much it is
I miss you. More than England, it feels. And like that country —
its half a life of influence in me as vital as blood or heart — I feel you
everywhere: in the vocabulary I use, as well as in the food,
and the poems of course. Even the breeze on Bloor this afternoon
sometimes insinuated itself, worked and twisted invisibly into my collar
so that the sound, the sensation was not so far removed from that
of your breath between my shoulders when we sleep, your arm
and its night-heat slotting into my ribs. The elements, it felt,
were conspiring to prop me up, keep me. Today, driving away
from the city we have made most of our memories in, the rain's
perfect descent was full of you. And a few moments ago, here
in a small wooden room, I recalled how you've been here before
and how the air might still contain faint after-images, an energy
that might be revived. The realization is upon me like a golden
and infinitely brightening cloak. I can look now in the carpet
for traces of your walk, your silver polish. And know, indisputably,
forensically, it's there somewhere. Just as you are, though far north
and obscured by dark greenery and a wash, I'll bet, of woodsmoke.

HEADING

We're heading Hopewards, homewards (even though
where that is grows foggy hereabouts, is a headland
all hazard lights and sudden dropoff), and it's cloudy. But
sight-clearing climbs are before us, then subsequent long
and light-on-the-gas sailings into valleys thick with fruit, pale
desert waters winding seaward. And just forget it, the urge
in you to find this happiness somehow beneath whatever
it was you felt bringing the paper in, maybe, or fishing
toast from between elements. Fleeting and predictable
passes through a blissed-out landscape might be all there
is for most of us. And why not, when it's so completely
filling of a mind dumbly preoccupied last couple of days.
Your left leg up on the seat, for instance. Its trim geometry
foreshadows the mountains. Also provoked are thoughts
on the sometime scalable peaks of your knees, long
brown slopes of thigh. A fruitstand side of the road
provides raspberries you take from my hand, all tongue
brush on palm and incidental rub of tooth, a bright-eyed
wink. Rugged landscapes collapse around these bright signs,
are rendered floodplain. And insistent surf-rushes of you,
what you do, plunge through a brain's highwire grey gorges.

ANNA KARENINA

Lakeside it is all beach-brown and soft lengths of you,
stretched out on hippie blankets we haul down steps
from the cabin. There are also the limpet-seeming and
mussel-shell black splashes of our swimsuits, some
yellowed sections of the *The Globe* we pass back and forth.
Beneath us there are fish that rise like reflections of your
dipping silver and alluring toes. In the middle distance:
islands I dream we might live on, hide a moment away
from the world, or even a full afternoon. At one point,
from the blue and serene backdrop of Loughborough,
its gentle mirror surface, its occasional lifting wave, your
hand angles in idly. Without, I think, motive or even conscious
thought. It caresses a second my shin, my knee. Moves out
again to turn pages of your book. And I am as moved,
I believe, by that gesture as you can be by anything in those
eight hundred pages. A blood tide rushes me and fish dart
through, illuminate with silver the chest's booming cavern,
and weed flutters tease the bottom edge of my humid, solid heart.

UNDERGROUND FILM

Whenever I head for the park and sprawl there, flat out
and full of your letters, those quick narratives of northern
work and sleep deprivation, or pay a few bucks to watch
a film alone at the Cumberland, my jacket cloaking
the empty seat, I hear also the trains that run beneath
and rattle this city. Last week the theatre shook
(sympathetically, it felt) as a Russian man who reminded
me of Robbie Robertson hired someone to finish him off,
so forlorn was he at losing his lover. And I thought, that
could be me, though his moves were amplified beyond
all reasonable action and consequence. I guess the conceit
I'm getting at is that news of my sadness and your unknowable
remove travels from one place to another by rail. It hangs
onto the smeared chrome, crowds into the yellow vinyl
seats. And as the weeks drag there are more trains carrying
more news. A teeming rush hour of absence. The ground
riddled, rendered weak with new tunnnels, and each of them
closer to the surface. More than this, at night and
staring absently into office-strewn sky, I see train windows
crammed with our remembered laughters and intimacies
as they stream further into the past. Lines of people on
their front steps weep madly into aprons and work-worn
hands at the news, the grim details of our trial. Even now,
as I finish these few lines, I hear another engine pull away.
And any minute, just down the road, European movie stars
will shiver and shimmy onscreen, lose very slightly their edge
in the face of such newly true and painful narratives.

STORM

Enough of this. Although I've enjoyed
more than I should the downed trees
and rifle reports as great limbs crashed
away, an army helicopter angling all hours
over townhouses, fireplaces surrounded and beset
by wind howling in — that dullish inventory
of a crisis. A woman on the radio claimed
to have found proof in diminished forests that
a similar climatic wig-out hasn't happened
in five hundred years — the entire lifespan
of old growth. Something shows up in the rings,
she said, but I tuned in too late and got
only how weather leaves scars, and noted that
her voice wavered, her bottom lip most surely
trembled. But I will mark this time differently,
by how into its creaking and severe folds
S. disappeared, the telephone lines severed,
or weighted so close to the ground that the fibre optic
appeared as an abandoned tightrope over highway 38.
I should take her there, point out my efforts
to communicate, my calls to her number littering
the ice- and erratic-filled fields near Harrowsmith:
a toppled three, a couple of divided twos, an eight
like twin neglected wheels of summer hay.
I imagine there are sheep across the road,
filthy, their feet split by winter and milling
loosely about. But listen. It kept me from her,
was a barrier I wanted away as if it were
a bitter drunk in winter's doorway. Which sounds,
even putting it down, a bit fierce, chaotic.
But the echo of her slim involvement in my
comings and goings fills already this room
and when (the admission makes me burn) mid-storm

the dry wood ran out, fizzled darkly, I ran
through her catalogue of bright words, her
brilliant shoulders, and found then its naked
hum to be also warming and very nearly enough.

RESUSCITATION

It's just another decent day, is how it feels, trudging along
mostly oblivious and wrapped in moderate happinesses
that shift intermittently towards even more positive
positions, and also through a couple inches of brilliant March
snow; Durrell's lemon and irregular sun breaking through,
or often threatening. A few bikes, even, weaving madly.
I'm on my way (and this just isn't news) to check the post
box for notices common sense dictates won't show
for some days, maybe weeks yet. But nothing lately
screws with that early-day routine, the obsessive and
banal frustrations of it, walks justified in the name of ambition.
(Though S. would likely — and more properly — link it to
something, ingrained in me, akin to entitlement.) She's on
campus this morning, resuscitating dummies, smacking
on their hard pink and cut chests with the heel of a hand.
Their unchanging and surprised, dazed faces; round,
worn-out mouths. Might come in handy, this first-aid
training, when we split in May, deal with a distance,
wedged massive, that could ride roughshod over us. And
things, moreover, have been rough past couple of days.
The urge is to drag up kinder euphemisms, I guess,
but rocky nails it. A better, more complicated truth
is that as I stand, key in hand, before a wall of boxes
stretching away towards the lake like some steel war
memorial, or a mortuary reserved, nightmarishly, for children,
I get how different is the touch passed between us this
morning, as well as the rushed and still permanently etched
kiss, from any that she'll practice all day, half the summer
without me. The terrain levels, becomes fluid and calm
knowing it's not resuscitation we need at all. For me it's
thoughts of side-zippered boots, or her arms arranged
symmetrically above, rest of her body abandoned (and mine its
willing shadow) night after night, given over to experience

and talks unheard of. This too, and most engagingly: the
cold-night bonfire of ideas and infinite refinements raging
up top. These revive me, as do a hundred other bright details
I've slowly catalogued (this is what, number 15?) There's
nothing comparable to this in any lessons can be taught
over two days, in cream-walled classrooms, or heard through
rubbernecked stethoscope. And here the sun, cliché be damned,
breaks through grinning, or did minutes ago, mid-stream
and so going unnoticed. Regardless, it is a mirror of me.

AN EFFECT I BELIEVE

I could hang around these places all day, and scan
every hour that hectic descending vee of street
for signs of her near-musical movement through
a crowd, an effect I believe stemming from the perfect
horizon of her shoulders, the dramatic and pure rise
of her throat, although once said it's adamantly not
so simple, is more theoretical, involves some minute
arrangement of deep-body cells and inclinations
we won't get the hang of in my lifetime. But she
wouldn't want that and, truth is, the metronome in me
swings wildly, pleasingly away from anything might be
described as need. Today I revisited poems of Don Coles;
they embrace me much as I hope and fondly imagine Sam doing
once power returns to our lost city. I'm daunted by the man's
stuff, all those still-intimate signals flaring in the brain
like high-school magnesium. And I see his loves almost
as clearly, even twenty years on, as I see Sam, not a week
removed, but some winding treacherous miles. And I
suppose that's why I wait at all: it gives me reason to
scribble, to ransack the inventory for a few hesitant,
sheepish lines which might, in a distant, uncertain future,
move her to remember fondly, synapses gunning, this
ardent time. Most ambitiously, I envision my efforts
staggering Sam, just as I am reeled when reading again
Sometimes All Over, huddled cold over a thin lentil soup
and some dire thoughts of these four days without her.

YOU

I'm drinking coffee on College somewhere
and feeling more comfortable
each time I venture this way,
though the cross streets still
                              elude me.

I would have thought
this bombardment of things
not seen before
                       (or else seen, but not lived among,
been part of)
was constant enough today
that sad thoughts of you —
the potent cocktail
that gets mixed inside me
sometimes,
              shaken
into my system —
might be postponed.

As further insulation there was even, this
morning, a decent review
of the stories in *The Globe*,
and at the next table a man
                              reading it
with apparent interest.
But no.

There is a persistent vision of you
way north and ensconced
perhaps at the Seattle Coffee Shop
in your tortoiseshell sunglasses,
                              your tired hands

running over my name in the paper,
scratching idly at the top of one foot
                                    with the other.

And even more sharply than these things,
(those noted above and also
the myriad arm and ankle

                    tattoos
on display these parts;
the sheepskin harness on a muscled and grey
dog hauling groceries,
as well as the awful xylophone player
with one arm and
                    one hell of an excuse)
I see the future tangle of you
and me.

All else fades faced with frames
that show glad and momentous sharing
come July of some Veuve,
then a subsequent confusion of our limbs
on the coast, salt on your neck
and gathered perhaps
                    at the back of your knees.

I expected some of this.
Toronto disappearing in the serene fog streaming
from thoughts of you, for example.

But soon it will be the Pacific Ocean
                                    that loses ground,
its grand trenches and thunderous blue approach
muted wholly by yours

and the fluid sense that

together we might rise above it,
or shed our old clothes

and dive within.

ON THE IMPOSSIBILITY OF SEEING YOU

It doesn't matter a damn how early I venture out,
or for how long I roam, haunt the sun-full and
endless-seeming streets of Toronto. I still won't
see you. Not a hope. There are plenty of shopkeepers
about, their sleeves rolled up and rolling out reluctant
striped awnings. I even see myself, ghosted, rendered
see-through, in stencilled and spotless windows packed
with Italian biscuits, or bright-eyed fish, the rude sundered
legs of spring lamb, neck-wrung grouse hung in head-down
rows like bats. A girl hoses down the sidewalk and light
arcs, separates (as we have) in the intersection's indecisive
jostling air. Yeah, there are all these signs and beauties,
reminders to get on with it, to live. And I do. But never
once in the coming weeks will you breeze my way.
And that impossibility: of your hand searching out mine
(same thing with your lips, and the frequent lazy sunrise
of your hip turning towards me — so often and fondly
recalled, and that more than once forestalled anything
might be thought of as work) makes it hard some days
to leave the house. Mostly I would rather summon acute
glimpses of you from the dark star-punctured swirl
of our winter. Moments that have been carved in with
the permanence of woodcuts and can now and again
be rekindled. Only peripherally — as if regarded on a rear-
view mirror while fresh traffic piles up more demandingly
ahead — but still. They bring you as near as anything just
down the road, any of those so-pretty stores opening up
and full of nothing I need to buy, except a little later some
paper for this poem, a couple of stamps, and a decent pen.

CURVE

My breath returns — finally.
And along with it some measure of life.
It even feels,
        though remotely,
this division of two could improve our lot
on the coast, render many months apparent
and unified from there.

I see us winding our way back
amid the evolution of grand stories
we slot around dire reminiscences
and meditations on absence.

There is, perhaps, an aching pause
at mountain vista where we interpret
the yellow and bold curve in the road sign
as metaphor for recent history,
        then drive away
fuelled by how we made it,
despite the fear involved in saying so soon,
Well that's it for a while.

And not merely intact, but enhanced
by self-reliances abandoned to winter
and spring proximity, now rekindled.

Still, I'd rather it hadn't happened.
This room flares atomic and silver,
        fills up
when I think of you.

The effect is that of a bomb
exploding among flour sacks.

And a few weeks from now, when
you move in towards me
(and I realize you won't stop,
intend in fact to bring me down

                              beside you,
stay that close),
all else will fall away.

Backlit trees plum-loaded and beset
by the dry, iridescent flutter of monarchs
might come close (as would ochre
and wind-smashed coastline,

                              some stretches of lemon
desert sands rising to the sun and back
in great shifting drifts)

but nothing, ever, will top the touch of you
on me,
        simple sometimes as handing bread
over cluttered tabletop; other times
so tenderly drawn
                    and drawn-out
the breath catches in me permanently,
and giving gestures of yours imprint somewhere
beyond the reach of climate, or geography,
or the language available to me
this morning with you still

                    six weeks removed.

THE 811 HIGHWAY, MAY

I was forever riding the blacktop
towards Armstrong, or away.
There were endless deliveries
and drop-offs.

Once, aimed north, with you
trapped in a Thunder Bay meeting
(I passed the offices, saw shadows,
the steeltoed circle of men
gathered around to listen)
there was the sense I was
absent something, had left it
irrevocably behind.

But hell, this was nothing new, all spring all
the minor and fleeting emptinesses
had the same effect:

that passenger seat beside me,
its crushed blue plaid.
Or the pickup that died roadside
and was abandoned to darkness.

Even the hip-sway and golden pearl-streams
in a champagne flute could seem, in my hands,
a so-sad necklace of solo moments.

And weeks before, at a hairpin's midpoint
(a grey lynx crossing the road and another
waiting) I realized how hours without you
would drive me strange ways —

to poems, even idiocy, evidence

being how I scribbled this
through all the highway's blind spots,
its snaking Keystone curves,

hoping at high speed to get it down
before slick trails gave way
to an incomprehensible gravel.

ABOVE THUNDER BAY

May proves jammed with piecework, and there
is no discerning the mad route taken
north, or way to map the thinning roads.

The life-math looks a mad smear and scribble.
All the same, banged up and beneath
sci-fi skies, I clamber heaped grey weaves

of slash, muddle through the thick suck
of Heaven's marsh, speargroves of fireblack
birch. A delirious sea-boil of treetops

crowds the day's edge. There is an overload
of forest. But then, at breakdown's door,
your hardhat crests the rutted mud track,

a new blue planet, and precedes you marching,
as if home from war, in your skinned
seen-it-all parade boots, reflective cross

of safety vest. The spike over your shoulder
is radio tower, and its spider-thread tethers
divide the distance into assorted triangles,

make of this vivid corner a stained glass
surround for the vision that is you
(a long day's saving grace) arriving

precisely when, under these conditions
and trying to shoulder their strange heft,
their absent balance point, I hadn't a hope.

AMBUSH

I am riding shotgun
south to Dorion. Kid
to your Cassidy.

With my eyes closed,
or set on the road's
pluming red-rock arrow,

scouring its hedges,
the sharp blade edge
of immeasurable forest,

I can toy with the lie
that we are alone.
But a dozen more are

gathered behind
and together we burst
into the high-sided

white-light narrows
between dawn and early morning,
like morning's first jet,

its filthy commuters.
A grouse, prim, dour, young,
jabs at the air, pokes

at its soft invisible chest,
noses towards the high point,
the red dead-centre. Then,

spying us, or if not that,
at least feeling the vibes
in her fucked-up backward

knees, she points madly,
makes a concerted and more
streamlined beeline

for the wings, storms
the fringed green curtain.
What's more, swallowtails

brainstorming and aflutter
with all their new-day
discoveries are sucked

into the Ford's V8 wake;
they throw a brown-eyed
lemon tizzy. Buffeted,

inconstant, they come
across as interference,
a TV static, and suggest

to this tired sidekick
mind the closeness
of more serious stations,

moderate dramas absent
all these old plotlines
centred on what might

take you from me first:
dawn's hair-thin road
or an ambush of bears.

THAT DAY SLIDING

There are accidents on this road, same as any other.
Somewhere a woman limps through thick plots of vegetable.
Cotton apron bunched at her hips, its warm hollow ball

bright with beans, soil rubbing away grey. Her head full
of a summer cold and the sense she has inhaled too much
orange blossom, the bitter, haired leaf of cherry tomato,

its milk-fur and shedding stem. Further in, beneath this
apprehension of scents and the lime shimmy of willow at creek-
side, as well as the rituals of a life rejoined (albeit slowly),

is memory: a horizon that for so long was orderly beneath
the butter sun, predictable, but then loomed in lightspeed,
the smooth arrow of road petering. Then there are rooms

full of brace and support, false hopes. Later she stands before
the yellow moon of refrigerator light, a hand busy at her
temple. All the breaks, she thinks carefully, and all the way

back, are invisible. Her fear is another day without you.
And that day sliding into another, just as a car in winter drifts,
in deep-time, from ice road. Rages, roars, the four round

and rubber corners on it spinning through frost-gravel
pearls into ditch. Bottoming out. She knows intensely how
(when she loses it, remembers you in those desperately pale,

final arrangements of bedsheet, the breathless sighs into chaos
and flatline, and she screams away, hands too tentative
on the wheel) everything from here is a matter of grip.

ELECTRICAL PROBLEMS

After a storm I felt might take this cabin with it,
and when I've re-opened the windows, wiped
down chairs on the screened porch, as well as
the blue water jugs, orange bench and bare wiring,

I traipse generally about, collect and mend clothes-
pins ripped from the between-trees line outside,
and retrieve swimming towels fallen like forlorn
kites over backdrop pines. All the time so damned

aware of your not being here, waiting the rain out
three villages over. There is sun trapped in the twin
and curved aluminum rails bookending four steps
into water that an hour ago boiled, beat its head

at the shore, and which this morning was a mirror
we swam in. From the shoreline, its limestone steps,
I can hear the telephone; same thing some thirty paces
left and right. The rest of the forest stays the way it is.

ORANGES

Odd knowing already — a scant three days on —
that your pulling from silver bag two tangerines,
and us peeling them on Wellington, walking as
far as it took with them, the street getting its light
from what I felt at seeing their twin suns, is something
I'll never lose. Hell, think on it, the knowledge that
you thought of me beforehand, imagined in some fashion
that tiny parade of two taking place. In future moments,
however pristine and distinguished they evolve
(at a child's birth perhaps, or news of inevitable but
inevitably unforeseen deaths, and some personal
but fine-seeming achievements with books), this
appearance of fruit, your hand rising from nowhere
and juggling them, will occupy so high and permanent
a place as to feel an annotation on life. Or else
reminiscent — and this is both more and less concrete —
of the jet's stream that while we ate, with the same
taste flooring both of us, refused to dissipate
in a cobalt and near-seeming winter sky.

POLAR

There must be a better way than this. Though I've said
that before, then stumbled on. But somewhere there's a new
angle or way of getting at what it is in your effect that kindles
such persistent brush fire. Painting the stairs in our new place
today, for instance (something that seems so slight, so
unlikely a trigger), each riser caught the light and hit home
the same true tone as your Village sweater. And at the airport,
watching you clear security, the metal and electric wand
was a thin hand in the small of your back, but seemed also
intrusive and its silver line dogged me most of the way
across town. I stopped at the zoo — a way of showing,
proving to myself how damned big it all is, this system, how
it's okay I don't get most of it, wander, in fact and most days,
in thick fog, in some quick descended cloud (by now you know,
of course, how for me you fill this illimitable world with
the certainties of lightning). There were polar bears that
from the bleak and underground viewing chambers seemed
to paddle lazily but upright, to ride invisible tricycles. Also oiled
and black-eyed otters that through apparent torpedo tunnels
built into the water's green muscle screamed ashore. There
seemed in their slick-soft dance to be new designs,
some near unexpected and clear passage into glades I might
move to, or at least glimpse late-night when this week's dreams
of macadam runways burned in through orchards recede. But
I stand at the edge of those fields and, head full of the sweet
sense of you, your imminent descent, landing lights on
and overhead, it's so damn hard to want it any other way.

COAST

There are ways to see ahead. Or rather
futures loom as oncoming traffic might
on foggy mornings, and it doesn't take
any rare gift to discern general shapes.

The second image forming dully for me
is of boats, cloud feeding among them,
and gulls wheeling above, though that
seems something that should be edited —

the life in sea towns is settled, becalmed,
won't attach to my life, still so hectic
with rare event and circumstance.
End of summer I left James Street

and there was money's quick disappearance,
its constant wane, and I saw that coming.
Same for changing clothes in parking lots
back of the gym or coffee shop, the grey

Toyota's trunk open like a mouth.
All this is predictable, I guess, or was;
nothing in the scenes would surprise any
friends. But recognition for the writing,

and praise, the odd grant, were also possible.
And so was, if I push a little, a place
in the city with great windows and plaster
walls, a brace of orchids nosing upwards.

Myriad scenic adventures. But there's nothing
foreseeable about this: a desperately early
morning with fragrant blistering memories
still dancing in me of S., her undraped

stretch today for a hysterical kettle,
the neverending grand tumble of hair I know
dearly now the feel of, the considerable heat.
Her laugh and touch are a bright continuous

thread among my streaming thoughts.
There's more. Another minute and I'll ride
out to work in a chapel friends offered up
as sanctuary in the fall. And muse there

on joys available should I spirit away
with S., haunt for a bit old harbours
that resolve from childhood, wild dusty
parts of Wales. Coastline I disowned

yet see her in regardless, artfully arranged
other side of a wrought-iron table and
reading aloud from the *Observer*, or else
flipping through photos that offer us

together, or slightly apart but reaching
determinedly for each other across
a backdrop of cobalt sky, bridging all
the unimaginable spaces. And with these

roughed-in words I aim for the same
connection, and I suppose also to direct,
in some localized fashion, time's traffic,
root out obscure hidden maps that might

indicate how best to move from here
to there without drifting ever into ditches
steep-banked and veering madly off
course, or into other less engaging arms.

TOTUS TUUS SUM

I am in a new bookstore full of people known from elsewhere,
though elsewhere they are without the blue uniforms,
the William Morris waistcoats. It feels I'm on a factory tour
circa 1890, delicate sweat feeding out. Regardless,
I am there and books are in hand, the transportation
they allow is underway. I read (because it is Christmas
and there is a niece) of a Spanish bull refusing to fight, lolling
under cork tree. The woman who pointed him out lingers,
runs a finger over the pages and moans so softly that in another
venue one can hardly imagine. I register then, and from
above, the Buena Vista Social Club, a music become
significant to me. The source of its effect is S., in Cuba
now and beaming, her long- and leopard-legged mind
loping the city's broad and battered seawall.
This convergence, it occurs, informs my winter. It ripples
joy out from spine's centre as if that backbone had been launched
into the sea by her wonderful arms. Wild how this sudden
enjambment of Madrid on the page and Havana in the air
(its own labour practices) — the Latin world upon my life
with the vigour of a man who would wrestle me under, swim
about larking — is not enough. How there is still room for her
up in that chaotic and bony playroom. She is everywhere.
In Cuba mostly (and, truth is, out of mind a moment ago,
first time in a week) but then also and realistically here,
taking me as nothing ever has, from books, and a moment
rare even in that world, when nearly unimaginable links
are formed between text and the very air, notes moving,
shimmying through its invisible bustle towards me. How,
I need to know, was space conjured for her, what immense
folding or unfolding of atoms? I am at sea here. My head
at these thoughts lightens, is a bathysphere filling up, and
the world bristles positively with its strange intentions.
Then, unbidden, I hear again, floating at me, words from

the Club, old sweet-voiced men pointing my way as she
perhaps skips the long white curve, other side of the beach.
Oye se quemo, they laugh. Listen, he's burning.

ANJOU

In a sudden though not totally unexpected April blaze,
and from a couple tables away (the sight of you sometimes
obscured by an American newspaper snapped too angrily
into breeze by a nasty piece of work recently arrived
in his Beamer) your bright laugh travels near, as well as numerous
similarly glistening observations, observations unrepeatable
but which cut through blue and impermeable sky with
a decisiveness it feels I can rarely muster, though I shouldn't
sell myself short. After all, I'm maybe halfway through, that's all,
and it's difficult from here to tell how it'll end, how strongly.
Stranger things have happened. But I know I should stop looking
so damn hard, pondering also, and at such length, the ineffable
and the draining. Trouble is, if I do that, and relax a while
the upstairs muscles, it's a good bet the lyric ability takes a hike.
But again, the moment gets away. That instant being how you
unwrap a friend's gift, Sam, remove breathy tissue from a blown glass
piece that from here (and to all the world, even) looks like
a perfume bottle, catches light, rounds it into pear-shape,
plum-colour and mango, then pours it out like crazy, a scent,
defying in fact all the laws of gravity, of physics. Which is bullshit.
The truth is otherwise, full of commercial and significantly chipped
prisms and chemistry sets, diffractions. But what matters to this
mind, in its irrational curves and fond inclinations, is that when
I see you from a few yards, and out of nowhere, often as not
you are bathing as much as basking, the spring scene becomes
liquid, the air rich with fruit, and the world suits you perfectly.

SAND

It knocks me back, your unexpected proximity
on an afternoon so mild everyone is outside. When
you could have picked anywhere. Beyond the glass
door of this café they hurry, birdlike and burdened
with bags, still-red faces abuzz with menu plans,
statistics on ball players, criminal tendencies. As
I scribble this your arm occasionally reaches across
for bread. Or a subtle scratching impinges — your
fountain pen on letters, pre-stamped envelopes.
These things enter (and gladly, however much I
concentrate on the poem) my field of vision, dark
chocolate shadows at the periphery. Put another
way: the noise of your industrious Saturday
afternoon seeps into all the lines, laps at them
like sea-water unbelievably blue and rising over
sandbags, rushing untended and wild greenery
at a patio door. Air, I think, also shoulders across
this tiny black and lucite table, though there is no
scent to it, just a sense it is happening. The most
energetic of the molecules knocks loose somehow
memory's door, those seconds this morning when
you reached for the venetian blind, blindsided me
with your dark stomach, waylaid our morning a while
— a time we also talked about coming downtown.
How damn different this is from anything gone before,
and how it staggers me the further in I get. But again
I stray. You are across from me and I love the green,
reflective, industrial-seeming fabric of your shirt,
your eyes that last night, middle of an evening packed
with less medical intimacies, filled up with a grit
both glassy and cubed, a rock we dug at gingerly.
Sand, it seemed, which links again to the ocean water,
the rippling depth-charge boom of your presence

in my world, or me in yours. Your hand this instant
rests on the edge of my horizon like an oar that might
sweep through water evaporated, urge the poem
on and, with its secular grace, move me also.

THE PINE ROOM

I had driven those roads before, consoled myself
with their abundant illustrations and footnotes.
There is a sense still in the air of mile-deep ice
masses; erratics range about hillsides like scouts,
but also like memories that have drifted away
from context's anchor. And I've relied a long time
on this scratched-up land for images dug from
deeper stuff than the city offers, though it feels
most often and obscurely that's where I belong.
But I never expected such glad excuse to pause
a while in an old pine room, its perfect wood
and gracious lines beyond anything I thought
was likely held in store for me. Same goes for
the bleached and leaning fence that staggers
away from the front windows, its pointed rhythms,
and the winding water ribbon out back. Most
glorious of all the signs was S., who moved
smoothly, nearly unheard, over white-bottomed
bedroom floorboards while I, from beneath, traced her
back and forth, spied light occasionally knifing
through. I knew she would descend eventually
the small back staircase, and that my wishing it so
had no effect. In the same way I couldn't persuade
a grey rabbit that arced madly both in and above
snowdrifts to not risk the road, its brief Sunday
rush hour suggesting there must be, further along,
a village church. My own devotion these past weeks
is aimed more locally: at S., dressing by then and
perhaps casting a discerning, more familiar gaze
than mine over the same country. In mind's eye
she idly, or less so, stretched a slim black strap
onto a brown shoulder. And the apprehension of that
last thought, its infinite electricity, was more potent

in my world, more poem-stopping, than all the
retreated blue ice, or secondary and odd-seeming
thoughts of how these brooding granite figures might
choose one day to lurch irresistibly and heavily my way,
or the house to fill up with half-expected ghosts.

BEETLE

Nothing to be examined too closely, is how this
new union feels — so panoramic, worthy and oceangoing;
each day these days throws off such supple surprises.
This is so very different from saying it doesn't stand
up to scrutiny. Rather, in these lines scribbled first, as now,
on a canary-yellow pad and later laboured at length
on S.'s laptop, or on the old clone buzzing away all decrepit
in the chapel attic way out on Highway 2 (a friend's home
and a reference not much use to anyone other than the half-dozen
privy to certain sad scenes, and to show I guess through
its fortuitous limestone history that movement in and of me from
the profane to more secular but sacred gestures) I hunt the region
in me that S. inhabits, the plum site her effect has settled in.
It's a proximity I aim for, an observation slightly better than general,
a bonelike and bleached wood fence I might build around a few
mental fields, sets of notions peculiar to this time I find it
possible to fall hard again. Thoughts stampede exotically
about, make such wondrous and unheard noises. And this
is not at all akin to the scientific process where the iridescent
wing cells and mothy patterns of monarch, the great white
blinking and blind twin eyes of swallowtail are trapped
under glass bars (or the jet reflective wings when she beetles
above, afterwards, both of us spent, her legs tucked along my ribs,
the wisp-fort of her hair a beekeeper's mask). I am envious
of that pure science, its clean breaks, perfect shards, but settle
gladly, wildly, for this rougher tramp through unknown
country which reminds me in its exploratory rushes of coming —
those first, adolescent and tentative days — to this country,
its innumerable sense-flooding surprises.

PARTING GIFT

Typing with this spiral ring of yours on is a striking, strange
procedure. The infinitely slight weight gain is probably not
root of the difference. More likely it's the silver peripheral glint
and distraction, that glimpse of a winding bright road always
leading somehow to you. A route that will be more difficult
to discern soon, with the distance between us amplified
beyond all noise and recognition. My memory of the far north,
its rough scrub and prehistory, its luminous and dark canopies,
is remote, fervently removed from the fluorescent spaces
we've inhabited the last few months; it's hard to place us
up there. There are a few pictures lying around of you, I guess,
and last night you found a little solace in trying on the uniform:
a soft brown fleece, the platinum head scarf — and why not
dress it up? But it was then the sadness, the truth, the plain fact
of your imminent departure, your quick rumble to the highway
and away, hit home, sank into me like an angler's lead weight
plunging through clear and rushing water. And just now.
You left — for the gallery, and only with your silver bag
(and around that, in orbit, the tiny matching planets that are
your painted toes) — but the violet and lightspeed rush of you
to the four-runner so clearly foreshadows tomorrow's bigger
departure, its desperate sadnesses, that this April afternoon
was nearly and wrongly swallowed up by future and fleeting
absence. I should, instead, collect strength today, draw on that
warm reserve, the permanent inventory we have stockpiled,
those memories large and rich enough to sustain me for a couple
months estranged, then a long flight to the coast and your bright
keening approach across an arrivals lounge, its ardent clicking
sign boards making cruel-seeming and cyclical reference to Havana.
The flip side — the inevitable long-term consequence of tomorrow
morning, or afternoon, whenever it is we drag ourselves apart —
is our quick reunion, its antic and real happiness. And because
it's what there is, other end of your ring's spiral, and ours, it's

what I keep my eye on, or try to. Like a decent and deep-breathing diver, I leap for the exact end of a bending board, aim at deep water.

POPPIES

Strange that nourishment should come from thoughts
of moving, mid-night, behind her, moulding my form
to fit, a move that in its design intended so little, but
had my head filling marvellously with images.
Last night it was a field lit by scarlet poppies,
their petal-wings fluttering against the bone cage's
inside walls, a sound attaching to it somewhere
between leaves over the road, wind in the trees.
But try to touch with the tips of your fingers
as lightly as possible, a nipple, say, and listen to that.
There was also, I remember, the tremendous heat
from being against her hip. Nothing in the four
meditation classes I took prepared me for the eternal
shapes created in that dark abandoned room. And it is
equally true today — I cradle still the absence of her
and the need to explain. Adding to the mood
is the way that Nina Simone is from the stereo exhorting me
to break down and let it all out. And each time
I go to shake it off, tell myself she's not directing it
my way, not to be an idiot about this, she says it again
and I flood with the difficulties of passing S.'s home
without knocking, or looking too hard through the kitchen
window, a glass sheet I moved other side of not a day ago
(although here, even with the faintest scent, the clearest
sense of her still on my skin, that seems impossible).
You were in there, I remind, and stumble on, but
add as evidence: there is a grand Millet above the couch
and blonde redhead music in the CD player. I saw them
at the Rivoli and made a story of it for her, her beautiful
knees pointing at me from the far end of the couch.
But all these details seem so unconvincing as I hump
through hip-deep snow drifts. They remind me of tabloid
dramas — the man who claimed astral projection

after a car accident, another's near-death experience
in surgery. I see cleanly from here, though, its desperate
mountain vantage, that everything is true, all we've done
is true as well as pure. And all the hard-luck stories,
the lost amnesiacs? Every one of them knew me.

THREE HAIKU

Nights without you are
cold, capable of pulling
me awake. And that

happened here. I saw
green and silver shirts draped on
hangers other side

of the room. They seemed
like dreams waiting for me to
fall, urging me down.

FROZEN

Perhaps you knew already,
and will realize reading this
that there must be so many things
we didn't tell each other.
Things I don't know.

But I have found mangos frozen hard
and then eaten late, end of the day
(perhaps with a nearby tumbler
of Talisker or Oban),
the meat scooped away with a spoon
from the skin,

have the feeling in the mouth
of luxurious sherbet, dessert
unheard of.

Which is wonderful news, renders life
slightly more, adds another pleasure
to the roster already so laden this year.

Still, this is a discovery
we should have made together,
which is sort of sad, and balances things.

YOU ARE GONE

I pour two swallows of whisky
and head to bed with them
so I can write. There
is the beginning in me
of a winter cold.

On the table, piled atop November's
Wallpaper, is a blue-jacketed book
barely begun. I am pleased with it;
the many faces within are already
moving autonomously. Still

this noise, all this talk
of grand solitary rituals,
is simply a bluff, banal sleight of hand
and involved line
intended to disguise how

the sadness at your absence
has moved out most dangerously
from my heart, become a smog
that rolls through my inner cities.

All the main arteries — the scarlet
and entwined ribbons that hold me together —
are ablaze.

A flurry of the saddest words
wells up. Wakes me
middle of the night
with its whisper.

They are a chill snow in the mouth,

a white fog that changes
nothing. Every one of them
simply a way of saying
I am without you.

SEPTEMBER ONE

This morning, with some coffee, and weighed down,
half-dressed, I managed (though nearly didn't) the dozen
angled, uncut steps to the dock. I read the newspaper,
as well as some serious pages of a decent book. And
then I simply sat for a while, thought on how winter
shapes up so well for us, exciting, but also on how sad
you were yesterday. At one point your tanned shoulder,
or rather the outer defined line of it — as the day greyed
and I listened to you, or later watched you sleep —
divided you from the water in a way reminded me
of medieval bronze refusing the alchemist's mercury.
The sad you, the becalmed lake. It was nothing, really,
just a dim sense of things being in flux for you, not
having the sharp resolution your shoulder did, set against
but contained within one of the world's cream-soft
afternoons. Today, as I drifted, eight hawks assembled
overhead and appeared to divide the land between them
before winging apart. Along the same line, two herons
heckled each other all the way to an island. And then,
before I came to work, two sunfish rose to kiss the thin
divide, and eyed maybe this cabin with its funhouse
and watery walls, its moss-soft roof sliding rain clatter
onto upturned rowboat. A Gillian Welch song poured
through window screens that offer a million metal-framed
and diminutive vistas. Trouble was, none of those views
contained you, and it seemed the only important point, still
does. There was only the scream somewhere north of an
unleashed bandsaw and, closer to this temporary home, the
blind drone of a dragonfly trapped under the dock's dozen
pine ribs, those twin fish mouths rising again, towards it.

MAD SCIENTIST

I'm watching some TV, as well as tapping idly here. Taking in
the old tube's unfocused streams of banal, dim dialogue,
its relentless and swarming static. But drifting also to what
feels serious consideration of a lemon gelato beside you,
its pale mist-hum in your mouth. Does it, I want to know,
cool (in any way that could be picked up by the proudest
new instruments — platinum and multiple gauges manufactured
one suspects in hard American deserts, a dozen lab coats
dithering) or warm, in detectable fashion, the air trapped soft
between your skin and the latest in a series of green and ribbed shirts
that slay me, and have for what, four months, two-dozen poems?
With that question posed (and even now revealing itself as patently
ludicrous, as well as of ulterior and notably dubious motive) some
explanatory and conflicting theories rise up, coupled in complicated
fashion to dim English memories of bright wetsuits, science class
lessons on colour-coded reptiles. Regardless, given that that
see-through and breathable skin, that slim stilled zephyr, does one
or the other (though for the why exactly, believably, you'd have to
drag in the self-same scientists, fly them up here), I have to wonder,
humbly and altogether more than simply curious, is there, with
a bare hand and your citrus shirt subtly lifted, any way at all
for me to feel that?

FORT WILLIAM

I remember a pink-walled and pickled pine room.
We were working north towards Skye. It was before
we arrived at Easedale's heaving thick seas,
razor-slate cottages. A woman working the chip shop there
would, about noon, seem to hate us openly
for our indecision and intrusions.

I lay on the bed and tried to imagine that future,
just to see if it could be done, to discern
a true outline from the impossible salt mists.

Sam dipped into a pool of old Hellos, filled
my peripheral vision with Prince Edwards and I
wondered which of us was being more realistic
about the world.

I could hear people I had never met
boozing in the next room, tuned to
BBC Scotland's report of a plane crash.
A girl glimpsed her reflection
on the TV screen, a half-corked ghost
adrift over that charred metal field,
and it had ruined, she said, a perfect evening.

I felt strongly that all the world's
perfections and pratfalls were at hand.
Trouble with me was, I hadn't been to Britain
for twenty years. My brain was trying
to peer around all the corners.
There was so much to work out, all that past
to be seen. And for an hour or two
I thought I would surely go mad.

HAY-ON-WYE

We risked dark, sodden barns, dodgy floors, gone-
to-seed acres of old stink and soft dulling books
that, though I wanted them to seem as brilliant
libraries, constellations towering the way Skye had,
much of Wales, were instead (and sadly) simply grey,
their words run tearfully together. From our hotel
later I stared into the fields, tried to discern
England's border, make out some sudden toughening
(or would it be softening?) of the ground. Clouds
gathered like talcum at Wye's green neckline.
It was a slight moment, but distilled purely, it felt,
from the day's unreadable confusions. I mentioned this
to Sam, who laughed, said she saw it coming, had
been studying again the knowable way I perused a room,
its view, all the various aspects of its ancient
situation. All the while, she thought, making dodgy
and a few less-so connections, knitting them together
so that something more than that first simple web
might rise eventually from the swamp. Which it does
occasionally, though perhaps not here. I see you
and I know what you're up to, she said. And I believed
her, though I hadn't known myself, quite. Had missed
in that old and lovely room how I was attempting
a translation of the elements, some alchemy that would,
if I managed any untwisting of the unspeakable shades
around us, save me from those bowed brown shelves
we rummaged through better part of the afternoon.

HAIKU YOU LEFT AS A MESSAGE
FROM THUNDER BAY

You're on the phone. I
can't believe it. I'm calling
and you're on the phone.

INFINITE RADIO

I had a more clear and prettier piece in mind. I nearly always do
and would have learned, you'd think, to expect more of these
complicated stagger-steps — the knotted, the near unreadable.
I had made notes on absence run rampant in a body. Some
drawings in the margins. The shock, though, and more telling,
was the depth and surge of longing's river this time, the bleak
fever and all-out muscle fatigue. I turned to books, worked
my way through Brideshead, mostly because you recommended it,
and swam in all its bright if overwrought turns, its sharp midday
ways of kickstarting memory, improving for me my recollections
of Oxford, growing up amid its brown and cobbled intersections,
the algaed riveredge gardens. And it doesn't hurt, going at a book
that looms churlish, to realize your prints are on it, your warm
breath-trace and finger-smudge on buttery summer-softened
pages. But hell, Sam. The lime trees seem some scenes to fizz
unnaturally. And the shameless blushing romance of it, that
storm-tossed Atlantic crossing where they fall for each other
(although Julia does stride the decks oblivious, strong, and
that seems a possible clue to your affection). These were
devices I thought would turn you off. All the same, beautiful
stuff. And anyway, this remains just so much preamble to my
saying not a word of Waugh, or his drawing of city streets
I grew up in, affected me the way your call to say I'm
coming home did. And that's what this is about and why
it was supposed to be more graceful. The most smoothly
moving part here is the thought of you driving to the top
of an esker last night, standing on the Toyota's roof, trying to find
an angle, an elevation would reveal the phone tower, join
the infinite radio dots to here, this room where I sit, a stranger
to these walls, thinking of you, your so fleeting remove, your
breath on books I love, my love pouring into books.

STRANGE TO THINK HOW

In a week we'll both
be gone from Kingston,
driven fast north, west.

Taken apart.
But then in a month, two,
meet on the coast

and share some wine
that reminds us both
of blackberries, the same

Swiss chocolate
and is poured from
a scratched carafe

into squat tumblers.
Also some views
of the sea. Maybe

we'll wade from there
into deeper waters,
make our way around

bottom edge of
the snowy Americas, just
beloved you, and me.

EVOLUTION, LOOKS LIKE

I'm enjoying this intermittent rise from trimmed barnboards,
from lemon-yellow and deep-shag towel, then the three, four
steps to pool's curled grey lip, the quick head-first topple.
There's a slight push from the toes but not enough to qualify it
on any of the scorecards as a proper dive. And I'm adoring
that action, that infinite lean, its deafening water-roar, the rush
into ear canal of a new element. At blue bottom's a robot
that's swept, crept all morning, sucked into its bright white
and accordion tail the soulless husks of earwig, of beetle,
as well as something that yesterday stung my left wrist
between tendons and at so specific, so difficult a location
as to seem omen, precipitous. It's a robot that emits a tick
regular and metronomic, gives the alternating impressions,
diving within its range, of womb, then water bomb. But
enough. I like also how I'm strong enough — though maybe
we all are, and always, thanks to buoyancy and displacement
— to haul myself up onto the apron, see you lounging far
end with a historical though probably not historic novel.
And oblivious to me, yet seeming also all-seeing behind those
tortoiseshell frames. Thinking, I bet, that you've seen it all
before, don't need to watch a guy all vanity and tattoo
pulling himself from the water like it's Passion Play symbol
for evolution, the big move on-land, when really there's
nothing to it more than a few sudden, damp Rorschachs.
But about then (and whenever I see you) there's a sensation
deep within reminds me of trout leaping reefs of dodgy rib,
tails thrashing back of darkening skin. And that's an effect
must manifest in dark ripple on water's skin, surely, or snake
Cyrillic across lawn, become worthy of a glance at least, a
look askance, some enduring humid and towel-dry moment.

SPEED READER

It was winter's end. Streets teemed
with snowmelt's white noise,
its glassy babble and glow.

We took warm root in a café
and I bloodied the front of some toast,
drifted away within the casual line
of that action, its unfathomable dimensions.
I loosened all the belts, is what I mean,
made some space for the first
inklings of poetry.

You were working on your own odyssey
and tapped a snow of ideas
onto the low wall of the laptop.
To do with London, you said.
Which meant Bloomsbury, a war removed
and before computers, or even this room
so remote from my own start.

For hours, and happily, we tested
and pored over our separate mapless fields.
Eventually it rained: glass buds slowed
by unseen parachutes, elegant ghost brakes,
bloomed on the road's lakebound arrow.

Behind me a woman I knew, or used to,
before the poems took off, shook out
her umbrella. She aimed its silver
ribstar at the ground and pumped
its slick trapped wing, released
a hail of chill see-through rounds.

You extended an arm (I was aware only
of its cruising in, its level approach)
and brushed off this attack, wiped away
any vestige. It took a second and was
over, we were on to other moments.

But still, I took in, recognized, that
written somewhere along your arm's
protective and immediate flight
were litanies of meaning, rain-clear
tattoos proving nothing, I guess,
except nothing could ever hurt us.

MY OPERA STAR

Picture the unlikely union of winter
and warmth. Familiar patterns appear
on the ground.

Dark fluid ribbons that splash
past steep-sided snowbank.

Water's muscle wrestling the obstacles,
whittling them down.

I see the Nile's curve reduced;
the Mississippi's brown fan. Out front
of the liquor store is the Thames
as it divides around Oxford.

Our town's become a drab Venice
with this blowtorch warmth
heel-end of record snows.

I suppose one might read the water lines
as if they were tea leaves, or tarot cards.
Discern great unmentionable event
in flood and ripple pattern.

And I try that, but see few very precise
or even readable omens
in this muddy deluge,

sense only the flood that races
through tunnels of arm, legs
like mine shafts (ignoring all the stop signs),
at the surprise sight of you
puddle-jumping gymwards, leaping

channel seas of run-off.

You are light wave, or radio,
flash way beyond my knowing
how it happens — and faster —
through all the widescreen panoramas.

Chemicals in me prove a thing or two
the rivers can't: If this were to change
I would surely drown.

And outside, beyond this shape-shifting
paper and streaked window, a woman
moves her gaze from the wet road
to a light in the sky and she *sings*.

NEW YEARS

Poolside, but still dressed from dinner,
we waited for all the machined hands
to sweep past vertical. Mused on a future
unforeseen, Lear-ish. Some end-of-it-all
flash.

Thick shadows played on the roof, black
fists of palm. At the beach, rooted dumb-struck
cannons stared down the horizon.

A few early whistles, streamer honks, rose,
drifted antsy from the neighbours' lawns, the almond curves
of their driveway. And before silence could rush in
again, chisel some space between all the certainties,
I glimpsed designs of dark taffeta and patent,
patently indoor shoes, hot nests
of elaborate upswept hair.

Your mother broke free of the television's
gaudy midnight blaze and hold, its tired songs and dance,
to join us at better windows, those giving
onto bougainvillea that tossed their bloody,
scented heads in a breezy, no-brain boogie
while neon wheels slid into the stars
and flood-lit fountains foamed upwards,
filled the garden's rough black tree,
made nuclear its heart.

Those same fireworks boiled minutely
within the armour of fireflies we found
ablaze and dying in all those southern doorways.
And connected also, chaotically, to the inner
buzz and wondrous flare of these two years

with you. Nothing, I thought, burns brighter
than these things, nothing. But
only as we moved away from them,
and knowingly, towards morning.

NOTES

It seems too soon to attempt the precision tooling of poetry,
crystal distillation of weeks spent poolside. My mind's unkempt,
still chlorinated. Arrogant to think I might capture already the heart
of it. But the need, as always, is to write, and the trigger this time
is talking to Sam an hour back, hearing how Timothy sees me
walking through fire in frantic blistering hunts for her safe passage.
Nice, that. And mostly true, though no more telling than Sam's
unconnected offers of lodging, a few fond incidents folded
into the coming weeks. I'll add these to a list of kindnesses long
enough to soon reach England, trail me this fall on memory-walks
through routes nearly overgrown, or warm me when all is lost,
or seems so — unfamiliar hills rolling to the horizon, oak-fringed
skies, and a language that doesn't fit me the way it did as a skinny
kid, all scraped-up tree climber and apple thief. No knowledge
in that boy, though, of the white and elegant room I've slept in,
its insinuation and sound-hint of pool water, wave of marsh grass.
(As well as the more difficult to decipher dark wing turnings and
swoop of swallows cerulean blue and cream, screaming into out-
buildings, beams muddied with this year's and other, older nests,
the white Morse line of crackling infant beaks, hunched young.)
Or of Sam, all the confidence contained in her movements, all
the sun, her down-south swimsuit dropping sequin splashes onto
lawn, a pearly widespread dew, as she picks frogs from the pool
filter, coiled snakes or, day's end, drifts through shade with wine.
It's all nondescript, I suppose, in the retelling, but dazzling the first
take. It has me trying hard, in this down-the-road and bookless house,
to explain what I feel at this remove, describe how love, ineloquent
as a wound, dribbled from me into the grass we crossed most mornings
with cut and glistening fruit, arm-tucked *Globe*. How we settled in
metal chairs, no clear sense of where we were headed, or are now.
But sure that years on I'll scratch at more of these serious-seeming
and blockish notes, my painted-by-her toes stretched ahead, and
annotate further this well-lit season, its humid arc, its cotton swoon.

Printed and bound
in Boucherville, Quebec, Canada by
MARC VEILLEUX IMPRIMEUR INC.
in March, 2000